KT-373-597

ROBOT CITY'S GREATEST HERO,

CURTIS
THE COLOSSAL
COASTGUARD ROBOT,
MUST FACE HIS TOUGHEST TEST YET!

MIDNIGHT, ROBOT CITY.
POPULATION: 15 MILLION HUMANS,
1 MILLION ROBOTS.

AS THEY SAY IN
ROBOT CITY, IT'S
RAINING CATS
AND COGS!

RO-BUOY ONE. WHAT'S STORY IN THE HARBOUR?

IT'S GETTING WORSE, CHIEF. WIND IS REALLY PICKING UP AND I DON'T LIKE THE LOOK OF THAT LIGHTNING.

SIR, THE *LADY JANE* HAS JUST ENTERED THE HARBOUR. THAT'S THE LAST OF THEM.

DID YOU GET THAT, NUMBER ONE?

YES, CHIEF. WE'RE GUIDING HER IN RIGHT NOW.

HARD TO PORT AND FOLLOW THE LIGHTS, *LADY JANE*.

OK, NUMBER ONE. BRING YOUR RO-BUOYS IN. GOOD JOB.

DON'T FORGET TO BACK UP YOUR HARD DRIVES--THAT STORM LOOKS NASTY.

YOU HEARD HIM, BOYS. BACK UP AND LET'S GET IN TO DOCK.

YOU ALL DID WELL TONIGHT.

COME ON, THERE'S HOT OIL WAITING FOR US!

ARE YOU ALL RIGHT, NUMBER FIVE? YOU LOOK A LITTLE RUN DOWN!

I DON'T FEEL TOO GOOD. I DIDN'T EXPECT MY FIRST DAY ON THE JOB TO BE SO ROUGH.

PULL YOURSELF TOGETHER, SON. YOU'RE IN THE ROBOT CITY COASTGUARD NOW.

WE DON'T GET SEASICK-- *EVER!*

DON'T WORRY-- YOU'LL SOON GET YOUR SEA CIRCUITS!

I'M LOOKING FORWARD TO GETTING OUT OF THIS WEATHER!

CURTIS IS ALREADY BACK AT BASE IN THE REPAIR DOCK. I HOPE HE'S ALL RIGHT AFTER THAT SHIP RAMMED HIM EARLIER.

OK EVERYONE, THAT'S WHAT I CALL A GOOD DAY'S WORK. LET'S GET THE COFFEE ON AND PUT OUR FEET UP.

BUT IT WASN'T TO BE...

CALLING ROBOT CITY COASTGUARD! THIS IS THE OIL DRILLING PLATFORM RED STAR III. *SOS!*

THIS IS ROBOT CITY COASTGUARD. HOW CAN WE HELP?

WE'VE COME ADRIFT. WE'RE ON FIRE AND WE'RE LEAKING OIL... LOTS OF IT!

WAKE UP, BIG GUY. WE'VE GOT A HOT ONE!

UNDERSTOOD, BOB. I'VE INITIATED POWER-UP.

COMMUNICATIONS DECK IS READY FOR THE CREW!

ACTION STATIONS! ACTION STATIONS!

NIGHT CREW, REPORT TO CURTIS. *ON THE DOUBLE!*

HERE WE GO AGAIN!

COME ON, WE'VE GOT TO GET THESE CABLES OFF QUICKLY.

SEAL THAT LEG UNIT UP AS FAST AS YOU CAN!

THE HATCH IS OPEN, BOB. WHAT HAVE WE GOT TONIGHT THEN?

POSSIBLE MAJOR ENVIRONMENTAL DISASTER AND FIRE AT SEA!

CURTIS THE COLOSSAL COASTGUARD ROBOT!

30 MILES OFF THE COAST OF ROBOT CITY, THE CREW OF THE RED STAR III OIL RIG ARE GETTING JITTERY...
THE FIRE HAS SPREAD TO C DECK!
IF WE DON'T STOP IT SOON, PUMP SIX WILL BLOW AS WELL.
THIS RIG HAS ONLY BEEN OPERATIONAL FOR FOUR MONTHS. WE SHOULDN'T BE HAVING PROBLEMS YET!
ANY NEWS FROM ROBOT CITY, NUMBER ONE?
I'M NOT PICKING ANYTHING UP, CHIEF. SINCE THE MAIN TRANSMITTER BLEW, IT'S HARD TO GET A CLEAR SIGNAL.
THE RIG ROBOTS ARE MELTING, SIR! THEY'RE TRYING TO PUT OUT THE FIRE.
THEY KEEP ON RUSHING IN WITH NO REGARD FOR THEIR OWN SAFETY.

RED STAR III, WHAT IS YOUR SITUATION?

WE'RE ADRIFT AND HAVE A SERIOUS FIRE!

SIX HANDS HAVE BEEN KNOCKED OVERBOARD. WE THREW THEM A LIFE RAFT BUT HAVEN'T BEEN ABLE TO RECOVER THEM!

LOOK OUT! PUMP SIX IS ABOUT TO BLOW!

CURTIS, WE'VE JUST GOT A VISUAL ON THE SIX CREW IN THE WATER.

ROGER THAT, ALI.

START PRESSURISING MY FIRE HOSES WHILE I ATTEND TO THOSE IN PERIL.

OPENING LEFT ARM RESCUE CABIN!

DEPLOYING ROPE LADDERS!

GRAB HOLD, GUYS! I'LL WINCH YOU UP.

IT'S WORKING!

ALMOST THERE, BUT I'M LOSING PRESSURE.

CURTIS, YOU'VE EXHAUSTED THE EXTINGUISHERS.

I'M GOING TO DOUSE IT MANUALLY. LUCKY I'VE GOT BIG HANDS--THEY'RE FIREPROOF.

OHHH-KAY... I CAN'T PRETEND THAT DIDN'T SMART A BIT!

THAT'S DONE IT. THE FIRE IS OUT.

BUT CURTIS, THE DRILL HOLE IS STILL ACTIVE!

I HEAR YOU.

WE CAN'T LEAVE IT OPEN-- THE OIL IS PUMPING RIGHT INTO THE SEA!

LET'S SEE WHAT WE CAN DO.

PREPARE TO DIVE, CREW.

SWITCHING ON THE SONAR.

WATCH OUT. I'M READING THE SEABED AS QUITE VARIABLE HERE.

DON'T WORRY--MY SENSORS WILL ADJUST MY LEGS FOR STABILITY.

UNDERSEA LIGHTS ARE ON.

IT'S STILL PRETTY BLACK DOWN HERE.

I CAN SEE THE LEAK!

MAKE SURE YOU GET A GOOD REEF KNOT IN THAT, CURTIS.

I'M JUST GOING TO TIE OFF THIS PIPE. THAT SHOULD SOLVE THE PROBLEM.

THAT'S ODD... THESE MOORINGS LOOK LIKE THEY'VE BEEN BITTEN TO PIECES.

NO WONDER THE RIG CAME ADRIFT. WHAT COULD HAVE BITTEN THROUGH THEM?

DO YOU THINK IT WAS THOSE ROBO-PIRANHAS THAT ESCAPED FROM THE ZOO LAST MONTH?

COULD HAVE BEEN.

HEY--ARE YOU PICKING UP ANYTHING ELSE DOWN HERE ON THE SONAR?

IT'S HARD TO TELL WITH ALL THIS TURBULENCE.

STRANGE. I'M SURE I SAW SOMETHING MOVING... IT'S STILL SO MURKY DOWN HERE.

WE'LL NEED TO DO SOMETHING ABOUT THIS OIL SLICK!

BOB CAN ORGANISE A CLEAN-UP TEAM TOMORROW.

SO WHAT DO YOU THINK, CURTIS? CAN THIS DRAGON CITY ROBOT BEAT SMASH HARRY?

I DON'T KNOW, BOB. I'VE NEVER SEEN SMOKIN' JONES IN ACTION, BUT DRAGON CITY IS PRODUCING SOME REAL TOUGH ROBOTS THESE DAYS.

THAT'S RIGHT, CURTIS. DRAGON TECH INDUSTRIES ARE BECOMING FRONT-RUNNERS IN ROBOT DEVELOPMENT.

AFTER ROBOT CITY, OF COURSE.

NATURALLY!

REMEMBER WHEN WE SAW SMASH BEAT THE DEADLY GORILLA?

OH YEAH, WHAT A NIGHT!

WE SURE HAD A BIG OLD PARTY AFTERWARDS!

DON'T REMIND ME! I STILL CAN'T FIND MY SPARE FEET!

WE'LL PARTY TOMORROW WHEN SMASH WINS AGAIN. SO BRING SOME EXTRA FEET!

WHO ARE YOU BACKING, JULIE?

OH, SMASH OF COURSE. HE'S ONE HUNKY HUNK OF METAL!

CURTIS, WE'RE UPLOADING NEW SOFTWARE FOR YOUR LEFT LEG.

LEFT LEG READY FOR REBOOT, SIR.

YOU NEED TWENTY-FOUR HOURS IN SLEEP MODE TO FULLY REPAIR YOUR SYSTEMS.

NOW SIT BACK AND RELAX, MY BOY. I DON'T WANT YOU DOING ANYTHING STRENUOUS FOR THE NEXT FEW DAYS.

ROGER THAT, PROFESSOR. NOTHING STRENUOUS...

WE STILL CAN'T TELL WHAT THE OBJECT IS, CHIEF, BUT IT'S NOW BLOCKING THE ROBERTS RIVER SHIPPING LANE.

WE NEED TO KNOW WHAT'S GOING ON OUT THERE.

GET ME SOME RO-BUOYS IN THE WATER.

NUMBER ONE! WHERE ARE YOU?

RIGHT HERE, CHIEF! READY TO MOVE OUT!

FORWARD MEN, THE CITY NEEDS US AGAIN!

HEY, NUMBER ONE. THIS SHIFT'S BEEN PRETTY CRAZY! IS THIS WHAT IT'S LIKE ALL THE TIME?

JUST A NORMAL DAY IN ROBOT CITY, NUMBER FIVE. WOULDN'T YOU SAY, CURTIS?

SURE THING, NUMBER ONE. GOOD LUCK OUT THERE, NUMBER FIVE—I'LL BE LOOKING OUT FOR YOU.

WOW! ONLY MY SECOND DAY ON THE JOB AND I'M ALREADY TALKING TO THE BIG GUY!

ALL RIGHT, TEAM, I NEED SOME CONCENTRATION NOW. IT LOOKS LIKE WE MIGHT HAVE A TRICKY SITUATION UP AHEAD SO I WANT YOU ALL IN THE ZONE AND ON TOP OF YOUR GAME.

REMEMBER, THIS IS THE ROBOT CITY COASTGUARD YOU'RE IN!

YES, SIR!

LISTEN TO THOSE RO-BUOYS. IT MAKES YOU PROUD TO BE PART OF THE COASTGUARD!

IT SURE DOES, CURTIS.

NUMBER ONE REPORTING IN. WE'RE IN THE ROBERTS RIVER AND WE CAN SEE THE CAUSE OF THE TROUBLE. IT'S BIG AND IT'S GOT TENTACLES!

WE'LL GET CLOSER TO INVESTIGATE.

KEEP ME POSTED. AND BE CAREFUL OUT THERE.

WE DON'T KNOW WHAT WE'RE DEALING WITH. IT MAY BE VERY DANGEROUS.

WHAT ON EARTH CAN THAT THING BE?

AND WHAT DOES IT WANT?

IT'S PROBABLY THAT GROUP OF ROBO-PIRANHAS THAT THE ZOO LOST LAST MONTH.

NOT THE ROBO-PIRANHAS AGAIN, MASON!

THEY GET THE BLAME FOR EVERYTHING!

COULD IT BE A STRAY WHALE?

DOUBTFUL. WHALES DON'T HAVE TENTACLES.

NEITHER DO PIRANHAS!

DID YOU SEE ANYTHING UNUSUAL WHEN YOU WERE OUT THERE, CURTIS?

APART FROM A MASSIVE OIL RIG ADRIFT AND ON FIRE IN THE MIDDLE OF A HEAVY ELECTRICAL STORM... NO, NOT REALLY.

EVERYONE'S A COMEDIAN AROUND HERE!

I DON'T WANT TO SEE ANY CLOWNS IN MY GROUND CREW! WE'VE GOT TO GET CURTIS'S LEG REPAIRED AND HIS POWER LEVELS AS HIGH AS POSSIBLE, AND WE'VE GOT TO DO IT BY YESTERDAY!

GET TO IT, CREW.

GROUND CREW, WHATEVER STAGE YOU'RE AT, FINISH UP. WE NEED CURTIS READY TO GO--*NOW!*

LEFT LEG CREW CLOSING UP!

SIR, WE ARE TRACKING THE CREATURE AND IT HAS STOPPED JUST UNDER THE BRIDGE.

I DON'T LIKE THE SOUND OF THAT!

BOB, IT'S THE MORNING RUSH HOUR.

THAT BRIDGE WILL BE PACKED WITH PEOPLE!

CHIEF...

I'M PICKING UP NEW SIGNALS IN THE WATER--LOOKS LIKE OUR SEA MONSTER'S GOT FRIENDS...

COASTGUARD! THIS IS THE RIVER POLICE. WE'VE GOT A... A... GREAT BIG THING WITH TENTACLES TRYING TO PULL DOWN WEST ISLAND WAY BRIDGE!

I HEARD THAT!

BIG GUY...

I'M GOOD TO GO WITH WHAT I'VE GOT!

PUT YOUR BACKS INTO IT, GUYS!

HAVE YOU THOUGHT ABOUT TRYING TO LOSE A FEW TONS, CURTIS?

WATCH IT, OR I'LL STOP GIVING YOU GUYS A MENTION WHEN I GET INTERVIEWED.

CURTIS, THIS IS BLUE FLIGHT. CAN YOU CONFIRM YOUR STATUS?

I AM A-OK AND READY FOR ACTION.

HE'S ON HIS FEET!

RIGHT, LET'S BE A BIT MORE CAREFUL THIS TIME.

WE'VE STILL GOT A SEA MONSTER TO DEAL WITH.

CATCHING THIS GUY MIGHT BE A BIT TRICKY...

IT'S MOVING AROUND SO FAST...

I JUST CAN'T GET A GRIP ON IT.

BLUE FLIGHT TO CURTIS. WE ARE STANDING BY TO PROVIDE ASSISTANCE.

BLUE FLIGHT, THIS IS CURTIS'S COMMUNICATIONS DECK. WHAT EXACTLY ARE YOUR ORDERS?

WE HAVE BEEN TOLD TO FIRE ON THE CREATURE IF CURTIS CAN'T STOP IT.

BIG GUY, IF YOU CAN AVOID A FIRE FIGHT IN THE RIVER, DO SO. I DON'T WANT ANY CIVILIAN CASUALTIES.

UNDERSTOOD, BOB. IT'S JUST THAT RIGHT NOW...

IT'S WORKING. THEY'RE ALL COMING WITH ME--EVEN THE BIG ONE!

CURTIS, WE HAVE ORDERS TO BOMB THE SEA CREATURES IF YOU THINK THEY ARE A THREAT TO THE CITY.

UNDERSTOOD BLUE FLIGHT, BUT HOLD FIRE FOR NOW. THEY SEEM CONTENT TO JUST FOLLOW.

CURTIS, ALL THE CREATURES HAVE CLEARED THE RIVER. BUT YOU'RE ATTRACTING MARINE LIFE FROM ALL OVER.

WHAT CAN I SAY, BLUE FLIGHT? IT'S MY SHEER MECHANICAL MAGNETISM.

I'VE NEVER BEEN SO POPULAR! I'M PICKING UP SOME SIGNALS NOW-- THEY'RE MAKING A LOT OF NOISE DOWN THERE.

YOU ARE HEADING TOWARDS THE RED STAR III DRILLING FIELD.

CURTIS, WE ARE ALMOST ON TOP OF THE DRILL HOLE.

TRY CHANGING THE FREQUENCY YOU'RE BROADCASTING ON TO SEE WHAT HAPPENS.

CURTIS, WE HAVE LESS THAN FIFTEEN MINUTES WORTH OF FUEL LEFT. WE WILL HANG ON AS LONG AS WE CAN.

UNDERSTOOD, BLUE FLIGHT. I'LL MAINTAIN RADIO CONTACT WHILE I'M UNDER THE SURFACE.

I'M STILL VARYING MY BROADCASTING FREQUENCY AND PICKING UP RESPONSES.

WE'RE GETTING SOUNDS THAT WE CAN'T DECIPHER!

RWWAAAARRG...

CLICK... CLICK... HELLO...

GOOD GRIEF! DID YOU HEAR THAT?

WE HEARD SOMETHING, BUT IT MADE NO SENSE.

LOOK, ALI--ALL THE FISH ARE HEADING STRAIGHT FOR US!

MAKES YOU FEEL LIKE WE'RE THE GOLDFISH AND THIS IS THE BOWL.

THIS IS BLUE FLIGHT TO CURTIS. WE ARE NEARLY OUT OF FUEL. WE'VE GOT TO HEAD HOME.

CURTIS, WHAT'S HAPPENING?
WELL--IT'S A LITTLE HARD TO EXPLAIN.
IN FACT, EVEN I DON'T BELIEVE IT. THE FISH ARE SPEAKING TO ME!
HELLO, BIG TIN MAN!
IT'S CALMER DOWN HERE THAN LAST NIGHT. I CAN SEE MUCH BETTER NOW...
AND IT'S NOT A PRETTY SIGHT. THERE'S LOADS OF RUBBISH AND THERE'S STILL A MASSIVE OIL LEAK! I THOUGHT I'D TIED IT OFF...

THE NEXT DAY IN ROBOT CITY:

HE'S DONE IT AGAIN!

READ ALL ABOUT IT! CURTIS SAVES ROBOT CITY! MAYOR BACKS WAVE-POWER RESEARCH! READ ALL ABOUT IT!

WHAT A HERO. HE'S STILL OUT THERE LEADING THE CLEAN-UP AND NEGOTIATING WITH THE SEA CREATURES.

THAT'S ROBOT CITY INGENUITY FOR YOU. NO ONE BEATS OUR ROBOTS!

THAT BIG OLD WALKING, TALKING LIGHTHOUSE NEVER LET US DOWN!

AND SO, AFTER FIVE DAYS OUT AT SEA HELPING CLEAN UP AFTER THE OIL LEAK, CURTIS IS PREPARING TO DIVE ONCE AGAIN FOR MORE PEACE TALKS WITH THE MARINE LIFE.

EARLIER TODAY, HE HAD A FEW WORDS FOR ROBOT CITY NEWS.

...AFTER ALL, AS A COASTGUARD OFFICER I'M DUTY-BOUND TO ENSURE THE SAFETY NOT ONLY OF OUR CITY'S SHIPS, BUT ALSO THE CREATURES WHO LIVE BENEATH THE WAVES.

WELL SAID.

AND THE BEST OF ROBOT LUCK TO HIM.

THERE HE GOES, WORKING HARD TO ENSURE PEACE BETWEEN ROBOT-, HUMAN- AND MARINE-KIND.

IT MUST BE A DIFFICULT AND DELICATE JOB TRYING TO NEGOTIATE WITH ANOTHER SPECIES.

HOW DO YOU RECKON HE WILL APPROACH IT?

I WOULD IMAGINE CURTIS WILL FOLLOW STANDARD PROCEDURES, KEEPING TO THE POINT IN AN EFFICIENT AND RESPECTFUL MANNER, WHILE AT ALL TIMES MAINTAINING A DIGNIFIED PROFESSIONAL ATTITUDE.

THE END